Let's Take Turns

By Janine Amos and Annabel Spenceley

Consultant Rachael Underwood

alphabet
soup

an imprint of
WINDMILL BOOKS
New York

Published in the United States by Alphabet Soup, an imprint of Windmill Books, LLC

Windmill Books
303 Park Avenue South
Suite #1280
New York, NY 10010

U.S. publication copyright © 2010 Evans Brothers Limited
First North American Edition

Library of Congress Cataloging-in-Publication Data

Amos, Janine
       Let's take turns. – 1st North American ed. / by Janine Amos and Annabel Spenceley.
cm. – (Best behavior)
       Contents: Bike ride—On the slide.
       Summary: Two brief stories demonstrate the importance of taking turns when playing with friends.
       ISBN 978-1-60754-512-5 (lib.) – 978-1-60754-513-2 (pbk.)
978-1-60754-515-6 (6 pack)
       1. Courtesy—Juvenile literature   [1. Etiquette   2. Conduct of life]
I. Spenceley, Annabel   II. Title   III. Series
       395.1/22—dc22

Manufactured in China

With thanks to: Jack Hetherington, Reuben Rosso, Bryony Jones, Tayce Rickets, and Danielle Rutter.

Bike Ride

Danielle is on the bike.

Tayce wants it.

Tayce pushes Danielle off
and takes the bike.

How do you think Tayce feels?
How do you think Danielle feels?

Danielle feels sad and angry.

What do you think will happen next?

Danielle grabs the bike back.

Danielle and Tayce shout.

Danielle's mom comes over.
"Danielle, you look upset,"
says Mom.

"And Tayce, you seem angry."

"I want the bike!" says Tayce.

"I was on the bike. You pushed me," says Danielle.

Danielle and Tayce both want the bike. What could they do?

16

"Tayce can have the bike when I've finished my turn," says Danielle.

17

"I'll ride around three times," says Danielle. "Then it's your turn."

18

"OK," agrees Tayce.
"I'll count."

They have worked it out. Danielle takes a turn on the bike.

Now it is Tayce's turn.

They have both had a turn.
How is Danielle feeling now?
How is Tayce feeling?

On the Slide

Reuben is on the slide. He is going down on his tummy.

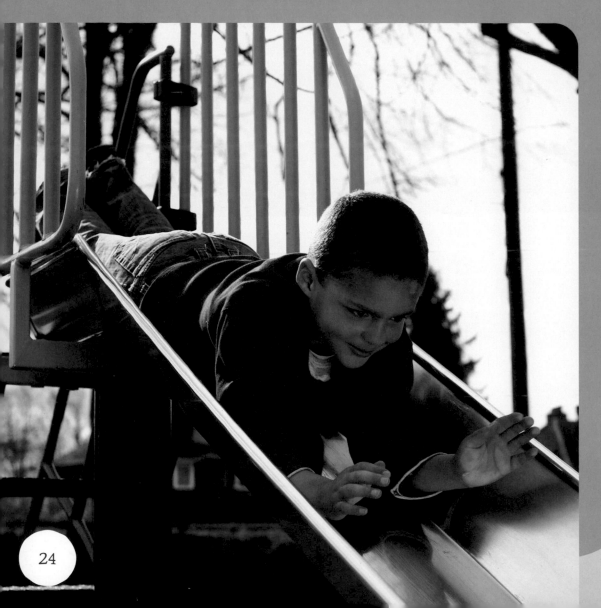

Jack wants to slide, too.
"Hurry up!" calls Jack.
**What do you think will
happen next?**

Jack sets off. Reuben is still on the slide.

They crash!

"That hurt me!" says Reuben.
"It hurt me, too!" said Jack.

What could they do next time to solve the problem?

Next time
Reuben waves
when he has
finished his turn.

And Jack waits
until Reuben is
off the slide.

FOR FURTHER READING

INFORMATION BOOKS
Krasny Brown, Laurie. *How to Be a Friend: A Guide to Making Friends and Keeping Them.* Boston: Little, Brown Young Readers, 2001.

Meiners, Cheri J. *Share and Take Turns.* Minneapolis: Free Spirit Publishing, 2003.

FICTION
Richardson, Justin and Parnell, Peter. *And Tango Makes Three.* New York: Simon and Schuster Books for Young Readers, 2005.

AUTHOR BIO
Janine Amos has worked in publishing as an editor and author, and as a lecturer in education. Her interests are in personal growth and raising self-esteem, and she works with educators, child psychologists, and specialists in mediation. She has written more than fifty books for children. Many of her titles deal with first-time experiences and emotional health issues such as bullying, death, and divorce.

You can find more great fiction and nonfiction from Windmill Books at windmillbooks.com